SOUTH BAY BARGAIN GUIDE

By Diane Brazil

Chronicle Books / San Francisco

Copyright © 1981 by Diane Brazil.
All rights reserved.
Printed in the United States of America.

Library of Congress Cataloging in Publication Data

Brazil, Diane.
  South Bay bargain guide.

  1. Discount houses (Retail trade)—California—
San Jose metropolitan area—Directories. 2. Outlet
stores—California—San Jose metropolitan area—
Directories. I. Title.
HF5429.215.U6B7   381'.1   81-2717
ISBN 0-87701-142-7   AACR2

Editing by Marian Petre.
Design by Suzanne Townsend.
Composition by Communi-Comp.

Chronicle Books
870 Market Street
San Francisco, CA 94102

DEDICATION

Coming from the north, south, and east, and over the mountains that separate us from the Pacific Ocean, settlers found this huge, green valley soon after the gold rush began. Its beautiful climate and rich soil provided a perfect environment for the agriculture in which Santa Clara Valley has long been prosperous.

Now, a new prosperity has emerged. As a direct outgrowth of the electronics and computer technologies in this valley, all knowledge has increased at an astounding rate. Some experts say that as much as 85% of all humankind's knowledge has been acquired in the last 10 years! This would not have happened without the aid of the computer to store, analyze, and furnish information. The creative and dynamic industries in this valley started it all and now lead the world in innovative and revolutionary scientific breakthroughs.

Our population has grown to over 1,200,000 and is still growing faster than that of most places in the world. We enjoy a harmonious and remarkable blend of races, religions, and cultures. We are a multi-university area with all the intellectual and cultural benefits thereof. Besides our many beautiful parks and rose gardens, we enjoy easy access to the ocean, mountains, and desert areas that make California geographically unique among states.

Santa Clara Valley comprises, indeed, an exciting, future-oriented area steeped in rich traditions and history. I, obviously, am proud of this valley—of its people, its accomplishments, and its potential. It has been a very gratifying experience to research and compile this book, and it is with great pleasure that I dedicate it to you—the people of this great valley.

CONTENTS

PREFACE

During a 4-year hiatus (to bear and raise my beautiful son), I was on a very limited budget, so I spent much of my time looking for best buys on quality merchandise. Thus, I discovered many of the places in the book. Friends who swooned over my bargains increasingly requested names and locations of my "finds." The idea for the book came from a desire to share the information with as many people as possible. In these times of tight money, it seems especially appropriate to go to extra lengths to save money. This book will make it lots easier for you. I wish I could be with you when you save a bundle because you've taken my advice and gone to the places in the book. Your satisfaction is my reward.

My criteria for the selection of merchants in this book were as follows:

- The quality of the merchandise had to be good to excellent. We can all find the low quality merchandise at low prices, but I wanted you to know where to find the good stuff cheaper.

- Discounts had to be 20% or greater. In some cases, discounts started at 10% off regular retail but ranged upward to larger discounts.

- Service was a criterion, but not the most important one. Sometimes we have to sacrifice a bit of service to appreciate larger discounts. Personally, I can live without all the amenities if I'm saving a bunch of money.

All percentages of discounts, prices, statements regarding amounts of savings and quality of merchandise are based on merchants' claims and, in some cases, my own personal observation. All information provided in this book is subject to change without notification.

INTRODUCTION TO THE SOUTH BAY BARGAIN GUIDE

The *South Bay Bargain Guide* is extensively researched, worth far more than its purchase price. Look upon it as an investment—it is! This book will be of unique value to the divorced or alone person on a limited or fixed income. The saving potential inherent in this volume will, hopefully, trigger plagiaristic efforts throughout the country to the benefit of more consumers in other areas. Read it well; it will stretch your dollar at least 15 percent!

> *I.N. Ingham*
> Board Chairman
> Consumers United
> Palo Alto

MONEY-SAVING TIPS

1   Pack your lunch as often as possible. You'd be surprised how fast those lunches out (even the inexpensive ones) add up and make a dent in your food budget.

2   Budget your money. If you don't know how, go to the library or a bookstore and get a book telling how. If you must, hire an expert or (even better) see an expert for free. Call the Consumer Credit Counselors of Santa Clara Valley at 286-8826 for free budgeting advice and more.

3   Watch the local papers for restaurant ads on specials and for coupons.

4   Go to matinees instead of evening shows whenever possible. You can see the first-run, most popular movies at about 2/3 off what it costs in the evening, and the lines for matinee showings are usually shorter.

5   Buy last year's model of the car you want NEW from dealers just when the new models are about to come out (or just *after* they come out). Dealers will mark the last year's models remaining on the lot down to the bare bones just to make room for newer models. And, by all means, anytime you purchase a car from a dealer, barter, barter, barter—whether you're buying a brand new model, last year's model, or a used vehicle. Read consumer publications for ratings on all the cars to determine what is the best buy in the type of vehicle you want.

6   Try co-operative buying of food. Pond's Products, for example, offers some very good savings on excellent food products bought in quantity. If a case of canned something-or-other is too much for your family to use, go in with a neighbor or several neighbors for these quantity purchases. There are many co-ops already established in this area that are making purchases of all types of food products and saving loads of money. Go to the periodical files in your local library for more information on food-buying co-ops.

7   Go to the flea markets. The San Jose area has several flea markets, among them the biggest one in the world, located on Berryessa Road. Clean out all that deadwood in your house and garage, and take it out there on a Sunday. There are approximately five times as many people out there shopping around on Sunday as there are on Saturday. So, if you're going out there to shop, go on Saturday to avoid the crowds, and if to sell, go on Sunday. You'll be amazed how much money you can pick up selling all that "junk" around your place. One man's trash is another man's treasure, and it has never been more obvious than at the flea markets.

8   Compare banks for best interest rates on your savings (no matter how meager or grand) and lowest service charges on checking accounts. Banks really are competitive and you'll be surprised at the differences.

9   Try not to use your charge accounts unless you can pay off the entire amount as soon as the bill arrives. Interest on unpaid balances usually adds as much as 18% onto the price of each purchase. Think about that when you're charging.

10   Barter for goods and services whenever possible. Don't be shy! Most people that barter enjoy it as much for the fun as for the savings. If your neighbor's a tax accountant and doesn't have time to take care of the yard, offer free yard work in exchange for the neighbor doing your taxes. The possibilities are endless.

11   Buy Christmas supplies in January. All Christmas cards, decorations, and paraphernalia are on sale in January and sometimes right after Christmas Day, so go out of your way just a little for these seasonal purchases.

12   Do your Christmas shopping all year. Keep a list (mental or otherwise) of everyone you need gifts for and, keeping in mind what's suitable for a particular person, have your eyes peeled for good buys all year. Saves you money and all that hassle right before the holidays. You can concentrate on relaxing and enjoying the holiday season while everyone else is fighting lines, high prices, traffic, and parking problems.

13   Look for children's clothing at Goodwill, Salvation Army, St. Vincent de Paul, and similar used-merchandise stores. Most younger children grow out of clothes before they're worn out, and not everyone thinks to pass the cast-offs along to someone else, so those perfectly good clothes are just given to the Goodwill, et al. I personally have found some very high quality children's clothes in perfect condition that way.

14   Have medical insurance if you can possibly swing it. As we all know, medical costs are getting out of hand, so the only real relief is medical insurance. Many employers offer some type of medical insurance. If yours doesn't, call the well-known companies (such as Blue Cross, Kaiser, etc.) and compare prices and plans. You will probably never regret that investment.

15 Bargains in housing are next to impossible to find in the valley. After all, it *is* a very desirable place to live (read the dedication in the front of the book), and there really are more people here than there is housing to hold them all. Here's a dynamite tip from Phyllis Drake, Real Estate Editor for the San Jose **Mercury-News,** if you're looking for a house to buy: look for a fixer-upper in a decent neighborhood. Make certain the house is architecturally and structurally sound. Look into creative financing; consult with bankers on this method of buying a house. Shop around for a reputable realtor. After you've found your potential dream house and have made the right deal for your budget, be prepared to put of lot of your time into fixing it up—then sit back and watch it appreciate!

16 Make your own home repairs whenever possible. If you don't know how, by all means, go to the library and find out. You'd be surprised how easy and rewarding many home repairs can be. Never, but never, try to fix something that's covered by a warranty. If you goof up, the warranty may automatically be invalid.

17 Take adult education classes for little or no cost. Learn to fix your car, sew, cook gourmet cuisine, operate a computer, solve a math problem, learn another language, whatever suits your needs or your fancy. It's so cheap, it's almost free and well worth it.

18 Buy used merchandise whenever feasible. I personally bought a slightly used, custom-made sectional for $150 through an ad in the paper, then had it re-upholstered and the cushion springs tied up (no extra charge from the upholsterer) for about $500. I have been told by furniture people that I couldn't touch that sectional or one of equal quality for less than $2000 today, even if I could find one as well made. So, as usual, let the buyer beware, but definitely consider used merchandise as much as possible. Give yourself a pat on the back for re-cycling while you're at it.

19   Trade babysitting with friends and neighbors—even for weekends at a time, if you can arrange it. Some areas have babysitting co-ops already set up, or you can set up your own. Again, go the the library and check out the periodicals for articles on how to set up a babysitting co-op. The librarian will help you find the information you need.

20   Carpool. If you don't know where to start, call 287-4210 in San Jose for assistance in carpooling in your area of the valley.

21   Don't turn the heat on unless you want to heat up the whole house. I lived in Seattle one winter and we never turned the heat on at all. We did wear two or three pairs of wool socks and layers of sweaters at times, but our cheeks got so rosy, and the utility companies got no satisfaction out of us! If you want only your bedroom and bathroom warm in the morning while you get ready for work, get a floor heater for that area. Why heat up the whole house? Be sure to turn the heat off when you leave the house. Call PG & E for more energy-saving tips. They really *do* want to help us all save energy.

22   If you can possibly afford one, use a microwave oven. Because it takes so much less time to cook in a microwave, it also uses less electricity. Makes sense, huh? Listen, after you've saved all that money on your utility bill by not turning on the heat, you can take the savings and buy a microwave.

23   Make it yourself. You'd be amazed how easy and rewarding it is to make your own furniture, bookcases, shelves, picture frames, and on and on. There are myriad books in the library telling how to do it, and most do-it-yourself stores give more than enough advice, so roll up your sleeves and enjoy yourself while saving a bundle of money, too.

24   Take up sewing. With a class in sewing (adult education or another source), a trip to one of the fine discount fabric stores in the area, and a portable machine, you can get exactly the styles, colors, fabrics, and perfect fit that you're always looking for in stores but rarely find, and save lots of money doing it. I have found that, many times, it takes less time to choose a pattern and fabric, then take it home and make just what I want, than it does to go out shopping all over the place to find it. On top of enjoying all the savings and the custom-made aspect of sewing, you might find that you really like it. Many, many people do, males included.

25   Save all your newspapers and sell them to the newspaper recycling places. Call 727-7576 for details.

26   Watch newspapers and magazines for coupons on items you buy already. No sense (and sometimes little savings) using coupons to buy items you never use, but it makes perfect sense to save a little more on items already included in your regular purchases. Sometimes Long's Drugs, for example, has double-coupon days on which all your coupons are worth double the face value. Since Long's already sells many items (such as cleaning products, paper goods, and more) cheaper than in many other stores, those double-coupon days can be very profitable.

27   Make a shopping list and stick to it. I know, you keep hearing this but, believe me, it works as far as saving money is concerned. Keeps you from buying all those impulse items that grocery stores go through all kinds of trouble to get you to buy, and makes you more conscious of what you're buying. And, for heaven's sake, don't go grocery shopping when you're hungry. If you can manage it, the best time to go is just after you've overindulged (again) and think you may possibly never eat another meal. And please don't let your mind wander when you're in the grocery store. Stay alert and stick to business. Spending money is serious business.

28   Compare unit prices on food items. The large size isn't always cheaper than two of the smaller ones—believe it or not! Take a minute to figure it out on each item you purchase. Keep in mind just how much of the item you'll really use before it turns bad. If you're buying for just one person, and it takes you a month to put away a gallon of milk, it will obviously be sour before you can use it all. So even though a gallon is probably cheaper than four quarts bought separately, that gallon would not be your best buy. As I said before, stay alert when you're shopping.

29   Check local book stores for bargains on many types of books. The larger book stores, especially, sometimes have outstanding sales. This would be a good source of Christmas gifts and something you can buy all year round.

30   Go to the library. Many of us (me included) have purchased books to read once with no intention of ever looking at them again. They take up space and are a waste of money when you consider that you could have borrowed the book in the first place.

31 Check the Yellow Pages for manufacturers of whatever you're looking to buy. That's one of the research techniques I used in compiling this book, and I found gold in them thar Yellow Pages. Just look under the category for manufacturers, and call them and ask if they sell direct to the public. It's so simple and sometimes very profitable.

32 Always look for quality. The absolute best buys are *quality* merchandise at a discount. In the long run, the "cheap stuff" falls apart so fast that, even if you didn't pay much for it, it really wasn't a bargain after all. The quality merchandise lasts longer and is thereby the best buy in the long run, especially when you can get it on sale or at a discount.

33 If you can't get into making it yourself, try the unfinished furniture stores for very good savings on wood furniture. In most cases, it is all ready to be stained or painted, which is a minor inconvenience, considering the potential savings. Do yourself a favor and compare prices in the unfinished furniture stores. Always keeping an eye on quality, you should determine your best buy for the money before you make the purchase.

34 Try all the catalog stores for good bargains on appliances, jewelry, toys, housewares, and more. Again, compare prices among catalog stores (and with regular retail stores) to realize your best savings. Locally, we have Best Products, Consumer's Distributing, Kessler's, and Service Merchandise. All catalogs are free, so get them all and look up the items you want in order to see who's the least expensive. Compare on each separate purchase, since these places are very competitive. No one catalog store is always cheaper on every item.

35 When you're shopping for anything, look for flaws. If you can repair or tolerate the flaw, and if the item hasn't already been marked down due to the flaw, talk to the manager (but nicely) about taking off a little extra. It doesn't usually work to discuss such a transaction with clerks; they have neither the authority nor sometimes the information available to make any additional discounts. Make certain the flaw won't affect the performance of the article or that the article can be made near-perfect with minor repair.

36 Eat less and learn about nutrition. Contrary to popular belief, it is much cheaper to eat properly than to torture your body with all that nutrition-robbing convenience food.

37 Get a freezer and take advantage of sales of food that you would normally buy anyway. If Chinese food isn't your forte, for heaven's sake, don't buy 52 cases of Chinese frozen dinners just because they're on sale. Stock up on all the food you already enjoy and buy meat in bulk, if possible. I have listed several butcher shops and meat packers in this area that sell at considerable discounts and offer even more savings if you buy a whole side of beef or a quantity of any meat. And, if you're going to have a freezer, try to keep it as full as possible—takes less energy to keep it cold, thus further cutting down on your utility bill.

38 Read this book from cover to cover, get out there and take control of the marketplace by saving money whenever possible. We really do get what we want when it comes to merchants. You realize, of course, that we pay for all those amenities and conveniences such as carpeting, piped-in music, service we sometimes don't want, and, of course, middle men. If consumers refused to demand them, those amenities would all fade away, and the results would be reflected in our pocketbooks. Nobody's going to go out of business just because we refuse to continue paying for the conveniences. Merchants will simply accommodate us by eliminating the unnecessaries and getting more competitive where it counts—on prices!!

Bargain Outlets
A-Z

THE ALUM ROCK CHEESE COMPANY is a fine

San Jose establishment that specializes in pizza toppings, including cheeses (cheddars, mozzarellas, provolones, and more), salami, pepperoni, olives, and tomato sauces. Though they sell mainly to pizza parlors and other restaurants in the area, they open up their store to the public on Saturdays only from 9 to 3. Enjoy considerable savings on their many delicious items.

ADDRESS: 215 E. Alma at 7th Street
San Jose
Map K No. 1

PHONE: (408) 293-9400

HOURS: Saturday only   9-3

PAYMENT: Checks and cash

AMERICAN BAKERIES— LANGENDORF DIVISION is

an outlet for Langendorf baked goods selling at wholesale and less. Besides the normal excellent discounts, you get another item free with every $5 purchase. The place is very clean and, of course, smells wonderful.

ADDRESS/ 1291 Old Oakland Road
PHONE: San Jose
(408) 286-1810
Map J No. 2

1695 S. 7th St.
San Jose
(408) 286-9600
Map K No. 2

HOURS: Monday-Friday   9-5:45
         Saturday   9-4:30
         Sunday   10-4:30

PAYMENT: Checks, cash, and Food Stamps

AROMA TASTE, INC, is a

manufacturer of delicious beef jerky—you will recognize their label. Though they normally sell to grocery stores, they're also pleased to sell to the public at a very good discount over grocery store prices. As you know, beef jerky is high in protein and relatively low in calories, making it terrific for dieting, camping, snacks, school lunches, and just plain good eating. Since they make it right on the premises, you're eliminating at least one middle man when you buy directly from Aroma Taste. Expect to save about 40% (my calculations). There is a minimum purchase required, but small.

ADDRESS/ 435 Toyama Drive
PHONE: Sunnyvale
         (408) 734-2660
         Map C No. 3

         3050 Copper Road
         Sunnyvale
         (408) 734-2660
         Map Q No. 3

HOURS: Monday-Friday   8-4:30
         Saturday and Sunday closed

PAYMENT: Checks and cash

ARVEY PAPER COMPANY

is a complete office-supply outlet also selling
janitorial supplies, all kinds of paper supplies
(including household paper, stationery, wedding
announcements, etc.), printer's supplies, and
some graphics supplies. Look for file folders,
pens, desk gadgets, and more for the office.
Whatever you need is here or can be ordered.
Discounts range from 10% to 50% off list prices,
depending on the item, and even more of a discount on selected merchandise. Quantity orders
rate greater discounts. Everything is first quality,
and satisfaction is guaranteed. For those on their
mailing list, twice-monthly notices announce
sales and specials. Expect excellent service from
the friendly staff and don't be surprised if they
offer you free coffee and donuts.

ADDRESS: 1381 N. 10th Street
San Jose
Map J No. 4

PHONE: (408) 288-9280

HOURS: Monday-Friday 8-5:30
Saturday 9-2
Sunday closed

PAYMENT: Checks and cash

RETURNS: With receipt, for refund, exchange,
or store credit

ATHLETIC SHOE FACTORY STORES sell brand-

name tennis shoes, cleats, basketball shoes, jogging and running shoes, hiking boots, jogging
suits, shorts, socks, athletic bags, t-shirts, and

sweatshirts. About 20% of the athletic shoes in their inventory are of first quality. The other 80% consist of closeouts, discontinueds, or shoes with minor cosmetic blemishes (such as a glue spot on the suede or nylon) which have no effect on the performance of the shoe. Though they never intentionally buy structurally imperfect shoes, once in a while they receive a pair from the manufacturer. These and slow-moving styles are marked down even further than the normal 30% to 40% discount. Look for Nike, Adidas, Puma, Brooks, Etonic, Tretorn, and other high quality brands at these tremendous savings. Sizes are men's 6½ to 13, women's 4 to 10, and children's 5 to 13 and 1 to 6. Look for women's casual shoes in some Athletic Shoe Factory Stores at similar savings.

ADDRESS/ PHONE: 1008 Blossom Hill Road
(Riverhill Plaza)
San Jose
(408) 269-9635
Map N No. 5

1777 S. Bascom
Campbell
(408) 377-9872
Map M No. 5

15545 Los Gatos Boulevard
Los Gatos
(408) 356-9754
Map L No. 5

565 E. El Camino Real
Sunnyvale
(408) 746-9149
Map D No. 5

1931 El Camino Real
Mountain View
(415) 967-9114
Map B No. 5

790 High Street
Palo Alto
(415) 328-9288
Map A No. 5

HOURS: All stores except Palo Alto:

Monday-Friday	10-9
Saturday	9:30-6
Sunday	12-5

Palo Alto store:	
Monday-Saturday	10-6
Thursday	til 9
Sunday	12-5

PAYMENT: VISA, MasterCard, checks, and cash

RETURNS: If sole separates from shoe, return shoes with receipt for refund, exchange, or store credit.

LAYAWAY: No

AVIS FASHIONS carries women's clothing at 20% to 80% off regular retail in many familiar lines. I found a good selection of slacks, blouses, sweaters, suits, jeans, and some dresses in sizes 1 and 2 on up to 15/16. All merchandise is first quality, name brand goods.

ADDRESS: 676 Blossom Hill Road
San Jose
Map N No. 43

PHONE: (408) 226-0953

HOURS: Monday and Tuesday 10:30-6
Wednesday – Friday   10:30-8
Saturday   10:30-6
Sunday   12-5

PAYMENT: VISA, MasterCard, checks, and cash

RETURNS: For store exchange or credit with receipt

LAYAWAY: 50% down, payment every two weeks

BARGAIN CITY offers a 15% to 20% savings on camping equipment, clothing, sporting goods, boots, rainwear, pants (all kinds), fishing gear, and surplus items. All merchandise is top quality, and service is excellent in this busy store.

ADDRESS: 260 N. 1st Street
San Jose
Map J No. 6

PHONE: (408) 287-3942

HOURS: Monday-Friday   10-6
Saturday   9-5
Sunday   closed

PAYMENT: VISA, MasterCard, checks, and cash

RETURNS: With receipt within 30 days of purchase for refund, exchange, or store credit if merchandise is in the same condition as when purchased

LAYAWAY: 10% down, pickup within 30 days

BEVERLY FABRICS sells all kinds of fabrics at 10% to 50% off regular retail. In this huge store, they carry quilted fabrics; upholstery fabrics; all types of wools, cottons, blends, etc.; a complete line of decorator prints (the kind you stretch over a frame then hang on the wall) and the frames to go with them; and all types of accessories. Their specialty is wedding fabrics, lace trims, forms for hats, fabric flowers and all (get this) at an additional 10% off if you buy fabric for the entire bridal party. Believe it or not, even more discounts are offered to licensed dressmakers, home economics teachers, and seamstresses.

ADDRESS: 1400 S. Bascom Avenue
San Jose
Map M No. 7

PHONE: (408) 294-8725

HOURS: Monday-Friday 9:30-9
Saturday 9:30-6
Sunday 12-5

PAYMENT: VISA, MasterCard, checks, and cash

RETURNS: Except for items sold "as is," which are not returnable, you can return purchases with receipt for refund, exchange, or store credit.

LAYAWAY: No

BIMOR STORES is a catalog store offering almost everything in home furnishings, including furniture, draperies, window coverings, carpets, large and small appliances, and more. All purchases are ordered out of catalogs and delivery time varies with the purchase. All merchandise is top quality and includes many famous well-made brands such as Hoover, Philco, Bassett, Tappan, O'Keefe and Merritt, Eton, Hitachi, and other good lines. Normal savings are 15% off regular retail prices and you pay freight charges.

ADDRESS: 40 W. El Camino Real
Mountain View
Map P No. 8

PHONE: (415) 967-3480

HOURS: Monday–Wednesday,
Friday   9:30-6
Thursday   9:30-6
and 7-9
Saturday   10-3
Sunday   closed

PAYMENT: Checks and cash

RETURNS: Factory warranties are honored

LAYAWAY: No

BLACK AND DECKER, the

famous maker of power tools and accessories, sells re-builts, closeouts, new, and discontinued merchandise at 15% to 30% off the regular retail prices. All items carry full factory warranties, even the re-builts (which, by the way, are rebuilt and/or repaired right on the premises). Merchandise is well-displayed and the staff couldn't be more helpful or friendly. Call ahead to see if they have the item you need. If not, they will call you when the item comes in.

ADDRESS: 1186 S. Bascom Avenue
San Jose
Map M No. 9

PHONE: (408) 293-7350

HOURS: Monday-Friday   8-6
Saturday   9-2
Sunday   closed

PAYMENT: VISA, MasterCard, checks, and cash

RETURNS: For exchange only

LAYAWAY: No

BREUNER'S CLEARANCE CENTER

is an outlet for assorted household items (that were not sold in the stores) and for rental returns. Among the offerings here are carpeting, area rugs, lamps, dining room sets, upholstered furniture (couches, loveseats, chairs, and recliners), bedding, stereos, and possibly, by presstime, large appliances. Most merchandise is new and sold at 30% to 50% off Breuner's regular prices. Rental returns are sold at 70% off. Returned mattresses are sterilized for sanitation purposes. Expect Bruener's fine quality and excellent service. Loading is free; delivery charges are extra but low.

ADDRESS: 1600 Duane
Santa Clara
Map G No. 10

PHONE: (408) 727-7365

HOURS: Monday-Saturday   10-6
Sunday   12-5

PAYMENT: VISA, MasterCard, American Express, Breuner's charge, checks, and cash

RETURNS: Ask at time of purchase—many items can be returned for refund or exchange, others are final sale

LAYAWAY: No, but they will hold an item for 24 hours, and paid-for merchandise can be stored 30 days at no charge

---

CALIFORNIA CHEESE COMPANY manufactures and wholesales fine cheeses in minimum one-pound purchases and under a well-known label you will recognize immediately. All cheeses are top quality and are offered to you at very big savings over grocery store prices.

ADDRESS: 1451 Sunny Court
San Jose
Map K No. 11

PHONE: (408) 288-5151

HOURS: Monday-Friday   8:30-5:15
Saturday   closed
Sunday   closed

PAYMENT: Checks and cash

CALIFORNIA SOFA MANUFACTURING COMPANY is a manufacturer of sofa beds, love seats, pit groups, sectionals, and cor-

ner bed units for retailers (furniture stores). They will sell direct to the public at 40% to 80% off regular retail prices. They carry a good selection of styles, patterns, and colors in velvets, corduroys, cottons, and synthetic fibers. Most merchandise is overruns, clearance items, remnant patterns, and style changes. Factory hours are limited for sales to the public, so call ahead to find out when they're open for business. Delivery is available at a nominal charge.

ADDRESS: 625 Nuttman Avenue
Santa Clara
Map G No. 12

PHONE: (408) 988-3495

HOURS: Call ahead and ask

PAYMENT: VISA, MasterCard, Gold Card, checks, and cash

RETURNS: Ask at time of purchase

CARPET MILL sells top quality carpeting and remnants at 20% to 30% off regular retail. Brands are highly recognizable and the selection and service are excellent.

ADDRESS: 777 Lawrence Expressway
Santa Clara
Map F No. 13

PHONE: (408) 241-4415

HOURS: Monday-Friday   9-9
Saturday   9-6
Sunday   11-5

PAYMENT: VISA, MasterCard, Gold Card, checks, and cash

RETURNS: Ask at time of purchase

LAYAWAY: 25% down, time negotiable

CARPET TOWN sells carpeting, linoleum, vinyl, and remnants at 30% to 50% off normal retail. Brand-names represent quality merchandise you will recognize immediately. Prices include installation—padding is extra.

ADDRESS: 877 E. Hamilton Avenue
Campbell
Map M No. 14

PHONE: (408) 371-3323

HOURS: Monday-Friday   9-9
Saturday   9-6
Sunday   11-5

PAYMENT: VISA, MasterCard, checks, and cash

RETURNS: Ask at time of purchase

LAYAWAY: No

CASH & CARRY BEAUTY SUPPLY sells top quality lines of beauty supplies at 20% to 30% off prices in regular retail stores. This large store carries well-known brands such as Roux, Clairol, Palm Beach, L'Oreal, Wella, and more. Senior citizens are offered an additional discount.

ADDRESS: 2465 Winchester Boulevard
San Jose
Map L No. 15

PHONE: (408) 866-1515

HOURS: Monday-Friday   9-5:30
Saturday   10-4
Sunday   closed

PAYMENT: VISA, MasterCard, checks, and cash

RETURNS: If the product is unused or has gone bad, they will give you a refund, exchange, or store credit

---

CENTRAL VOLUME BUYERS (CVB)

is a big, barn-type warehouse packed full of televisions, appliances, mattresses, and microwave ovens at excellent savings. Most items are first quality brand names, though they sometimes have merchandise with minor damage at extra savings. Here you'll find RCA, Hitachi, Sony, Sanyo, Zenith, Maytag, Whirlpool, Speed Queen, Hotpoint, GE, Litton, Amana, and more—all with full manufacturer's warranties. Since salespeople do not work on commissions, you are saved from the pressure to buy that exists in many appliance stores. They have a very large selection of appliances and televisions, and especially microwaves. In addition to all this good news, they are willing to negotiate—so make them an offer! Delivery charges are very reasonable, and they offer free 30-day warehousing on paid-for merchandise.

ADDRESS: 1815 S. Monterey Road
San Jose
Map K No. 16

PHONE: (408) 998-2906

HOURS: Tuesday- Friday   10-6
Saturday   9-5
Sunday and Monday closed

PAYMENT: VISA, MasterCard, checks, and cash

RETURNS: Within a reasonable amount of time, depending on condition of merchandise. Of course, all factory warranties are honored.

LAYAWAY: No

CHEESE is a wholesaler that does printing on t-shirts for children. They carry their own clever designs, others' designs, and will do special orders on request of just about any saying, picture, or line drawing you can dream up. The t-shirts are very well made of heavy fabric, and the printing is excellent. All shirts are washable and come in sizes 2 to 14 for girls and boys. With 50% off regular retail (additional discount for orders in quantity and up to 80% off on sale items) and an excellent selection from which to choose, Cheese is not to be missed.

ADDRESS: 1435 Koll Circle
San Jose
Map J No. 17

PHONE: (408) 293-9646

HOURS: Monday-Friday 9-4
Saturday and Sunday closed
Special Sale Days Call ahead and ask

PAYMENT: Checks and cash

RETURNS: Ask at time of purchase

LAYAWAY: No

CITADEL'S CANNERY WAREHOUSE sells dented cans

containing all kinds of foods (and some detergents) at tremendous savings. Ease your doubts; dented cans do not impair the quality of the contents. We've all bought dented cans of soup, fruit, or pet food in regular grocery stores. Of course, we would not buy bulging or punctured cans, but dented are A-OK and Citadel's is full of those. They carry canned fruit, vegetables, pet food, and more, at considerably less than retail. All purchases are guaranteed, and money is cheerfully refunded if you're not satisfied. Look for all the familiar brands and Citadel's own labels in this huge warehouse store. Also keep an eye out for sale items, on which savings are truly unbeatable.

ADDRESS: 405 E. Taylor
San Jose
Map J No. 18

PHONE: (408) 275-0410

HOURS: Monday-Friday   9-8
Saturday   9-5
Sunday   11-5

PAYMENT: VISA, MasterCard, checks, cash, and Food Stamps

RETURNS: With receipt, for refund or exchange

CLOTHES HOUND is a very large

and well-stocked factory outlet store for a major manufacturer of women's clothing. I can't mention the manufacturer here, but it's a high qual-

ity line you'll recognize immediately. The same
manufacturer uses another label for many of the
clothes at the CLOTHES HOUND, but the quality is right up there. They also carry a few designer lines and have a large men's department,
too. Savings range from 30% to 40% off regular
retail and up to 70% on some sale items. (At last
summer's clearance sale, I personally saved about
80% on a couple of items.) For women, in sizes 4
to 16 and 32 to 52 (large sizes are limited, however), they carry skirts, blouses, dresses, jackets,
suits, coats, and sweaters. For men, in sizes 36 to
60, they have shirts, slacks, suits, pants, down
jackets, top coats, and most accessories in
familiar lines.

ADDRESS: 3127 Stevens Creek Boulevard
Santa Clara
Map H No. 19

PHONE: (408) 247-2970

HOURS: Monday, Thursday,
Friday   10-9
Tuesday, Wednesday,
Saturday   10-6
Sunday   12-5

PAYMENT: VISA, MasterCard, checks, and cash

RETURNS: For refund or exchange within 30
days of purchase with receipt,
except sale items which are final
sale

LAYAWAY: No

CLOTHES OUT is a small but well-
stocked shop in downtown Palo Alto that offers
good quality women's apparel in sizes 4 to 20

and 3/4 to 13/14. Included are dresses, blouses, skiwear, skirts, scarves, jackets, slacks, and more. Some of the familiar lines on hand are Lilli Ann, Joanie Char, J. Raymond, Variations, Koret, Sweet Inspiration, and Sundance Skiwear. All merchandise is overruns, samples, and discontinueds at savings of approximately 30% off regular retail. The store is carpeted and well-kept and a salesperson is on hand to assist with selections.

ADDRESS: 180-B Hamilton
Palo Alto
Map A No. 20

PHONE: (415) 326-2767

HOURS: Monday-Saturday   10-6
Sunday   closed

PAYMENT: Checks and cash only

RETURNS: With receipt for exchanges and store credit only

LAYAWAY: Minimum 10% down with terms negotiable with store

CLOTHING CLEARANCE CENTER
is one of a chain of well-known outlets specializing in men's clothing. What with all the outlet stores for women, this is, to my knowledge, the first one in the South Bay Area especially for men. All garments are first quality, the selection is very large, and savings can average up to 50% off regular retail. Look for suits, slacks, shirts, sports jackets, sweaters, ties, belts, and socks, all in sizes suited to just about any man. Alterations are available on the premises at an additional charge.

ADDRESS: El Camino and Kiely Boulevard
Moonlight Shopping Center
Santa Clara
Map H No. 21

PHONE: (408) 984-1231

HOURS: Monday-Friday   10-8
Saturday   9-6
Sunday   10-5

PAYMENT: VISA, MasterCard, checks, and
cash

RETURNS: Within 7 days of purchase on
unaltered garments accompanied
by the receipt

LAYAWAY: 25% down with pickup within 60
days, payment due after 30 days

CROWN TOOL & SUPPLY is a

wholesaler of hand tools, power tools, some building supplies, plumbing supplies, and related
items. Discounts vary depending on purchase,
but there are definite savings on all items. This
firm deals mainly with contractors but is pleased
to sell direct to the public at the same great
savings.

ADDRESS: 660 Commercial Street
San Jose
Map J No. 22

PHONE: (408) 287-2100

HOURS: Monday-Friday   8-5
Saturday and Sunday closed

PAYMENT: Checks and cash

RETURNS: Only if the product is defective,
and depending on manufacturer's
guarantees

DAVID MEAT COMPANY

offers substantial discounts on all cuts of meat. The meat is cut right on the premises—this is a boning plant and you must call ahead to place your order. Service is excellent and so are the savings. Call them for ordering details.

ADDRESS: 761 Campbell Avenue
Santa Clara
Map I No. 23

PHONE: (408) 296-5414

HOURS: Monday-Friday   6-2:30
Saturday and Sunday closed

PAYMENT: Checks and cash

DISCOUNT MATTRESS WAREHOUSE

carries a huge selection of brand-name mattresses at least 10% to 20% off regular retail prices. All pieces are first quality and carry normal factory warranties. They also have frames and sofa beds at discount prices.

ADDRESS: 851 W. San Carlos
San Jose
Map J No. 24

PHONE: (408) 294-0715

HOURS: Monday-Friday   10-8
Saturday   10-6
Sunday   10-5

PAYMENT: VISA, MasterCard, Gold Card, checks, and cash

RETURNS: Factory warranties are honored

LAYAWAY: Liberal terms are negotiable

EXOTIC SILKS is a delightful surprise, reflecting the sunny personality and good taste of the manager. This small wholesale and retail yardage store is packed full of silks and batiked cotton from China, Italy, Thailand, India, and Indonesia. You'll find all types and grades of silks, including special brocades, palace dynasties from China, beautiful crepe prints, and much more. Besides the yardage, they also sell silk and cotton women's clothing (some of it made on the premises) including blouses, skirts, and dresses. Be sure to check out their large selection of handhemmed scarves and embroidered tablecloths with matching napkins. At this writing, they also had a few very lovely hand-stitched petit point purses from China, but these are hard to get (as are all their goods from China) and they don't last long—especially at these very reasonable prices. So when you go in, ask about the latest arrivals from China. Though much of their business is mail order and wholesale, they are pleased to sell to the public at discounts ranging from 30% to 50% off regular retail value. If you're a professional fabric artist or dressmaker, be sure to mention it as they will give you an additional discount.

ADDRESS: 252 State Street
Los Altos
Map B No. 25

PHONE: (415) 948-6811

HOURS: Monday-Friday   9-6
Saturday   9-5:30
Sunday   closed

PAYMENT: VISA, MasterCard, Gold Card, checks, and cash

RETURNS: No returns of cut yardage. Other items can be returned with receipt within 30 days of purchase for refund, store credit, or exchange.

LAYAWAY: No

FABRIC WAREHOUSE is a

huge outlet for all kinds of fabrics and sewing accessories at a minimum of 15% off regular retail prices. Additional discounts are offered when you buy an entire bolt of fabric, regardless of how much or little is left on the bolt. They have many sales for even greater savings and tables full of remnants are marked down for quick sale. Other sewing supplies, including patterns are available. Everything is first quality millends or overruns and the selection is so large you may get lost in the store.

ADDRESS/ PHONE: 3690 El Camino Real
Santa Clara
(408) 246-1644
Map H No. 26

2327 McKee Road
San Jose
(408) 926-3203
Map K No. 26

898 Blossom Hill Road
San Jose
(408) 578-1021
Map N No. 26

HOURS:

Monday-Friday	10-9
Saturday	10-6
Sunday	12-5

PAYMENT: VISA, MasterCard, checks, and cash

RETURNS: Some items are returnable; ask at time of purchase.

LAYAWAY: They will hold merchandise 30 days with nothing down.

FACTORY STORE is located in

downtown San Jose and sells women's and girls' apparel at just above wholesale prices. In women's sizes 3 to 16, they have blouses, skirts, pants, sweaters, jeans, jogging suits, ski jackets, and more. For girls in sizes 2T to 14, they carry skirts, tops, pants, dresses, and jumpsuits. All merchandise is first quality.

ADDRESS: 145 W. Santa Clara Street
San Jose
Map J No. 27

PHONE: (408) 998-3066

HOURS: Monday-Saturday   10-5
Sunday   closed

PAYMENT: VISA, MasterCard, checks, and cash

RETURNS: Ask at time of purchase

LAYAWAY: 10% down with pickup in 30 days

FACTORY TO "U" is a rather

unique discount store. Besides ladies' apparel in regular sizes 3 to 18, they also carry some maternity clothes and a large selection of tops to size 42. They have a very fine and attractive selection of ladies' wear from such manufacturers as Byer, Fritzi, H.I.S., Tom Boy, Bobbie Brooks, Bronson, Ms. Paquette, and more. With 30% to 60% off regular retail prices and the fine styles and varied merchandise available here, this is one place all women should check out. The store manager is friendly and helpful and has excellent taste. He also seems to realize how hard it is for pregnant women to find stylish maternity clothes and is doing his part to solve that problem—and at a discount yet! Most merchandise is first quality, though he does carry a few seconds at even greater savings (check the back room). Though parking may be a problem considering the downtown location, I recommend this store to women of all ages and sizes.

ADDRESS: 60 N. First Street
San Jose
Map J No. 28

PHONE: (408) 293-5355

HOURS: Monday-Saturday   10-5
Sunday   closed

PAYMENT: VISA, MasterCard, Gold Card, checks, and cash

RETURNS: Within 3 days of purchase for store credit or exchange with receipt

LAYAWAY: 20% or $2 down with pickup in 30 days

FARR-WEST FASHIONS is a

manufacturer of lovely, feminine lingerie sold to some of the finest department stores and to the public in the factory. It takes a little hunting to find the place and you have to go there during regular factory hours, but it is well worth the hassle. You'll find bras in sizes 32, 34, and 36; slips in sizes 30 to 38; camisoles in P, S, M, and L; and bikini panties in sizes 4 to 7. The fabric and workmanship are excellent and the results are feminine and sexy. Besides first quality overruns and such, they also sell irregulars at 50% to 75% off regular store prices. They make a lovely, warm, comfortable robe that I had eyed in the department stores for $40 and got here (with a slight flaw) for $10. You'll recognize the robe right away—it's a big seller in the stores.

ADDRESS: 1047 Elwell Court
Palo Alto
Map O No. 29

PHONE: (415) 965-1550

HOURS: Monday-Friday   9-4:30
Saturday and Sunday closed

PAYMENT: Checks and cash

RETURNS: No, all sales are final

LAYAWAY: No

FASHIONAIRE

sells all first quality women's clothing at 30% off regular retail prices. Here you'll find slacks, skirts, blouses, a few dresses, sweaters, purses, belts, and 14K gold jewelry. They carry a good selection of coordinates in sizes 1 to 15 and 6 to 18. We found the staff to be friendly and helpful.

ADDRESS: 1375 Blossom Hill Road
Princeton Plaza Mall
San Jose
Map N No. 30

PHONE: (408) 448-2500

HOURS: Monday-Friday   10-9
Saturday   10-6
Sunday   12-5

PAYMENT: VISA, MasterCard, checks, and cash

RETURNS: You have 30 days to return purchases (even irregulars unless sold "As Is") with the receipt for refund, exchange, or store credit

LAYAWAY: 30% down, pickup in 30 days

FUN ENTERPRISES specializes

in toys and novelties used as prizes in carnival games, including all sizes of stuffed toys, at up to 60% off the prices in stores. Visit their showroom and have fun selecting goodies for your own carnival or gifts for everyone.

ADDRESS: 374 Martin
Santa Clara
Map I No. 31

PHONE: (408) 727-9876

HOURS:
Monday-Friday	10-4
Saturday	by appointment
Sunday	closed

PAYMENT: VISA, MasterCard, checks, and cash

GE SERVICENTER services and

sells portable appliances and audio equipment. The merchandise is new but found defective—sometimes before it reaches the stores. The Servicenter takes the defective item, reconditions or repairs it, then sells it at 15% to 30% off normal retail, *and* with the same factory warranties as originally first quality merchandise. They specialize in portable appliances such as toasters, broiler ovens, irons, coffee pots, etc., and also carry audio equipment. Remember, this is not *used* then rebuilt merchandise. It is brand new with minor defects that have been repaired. They also sell closeouts and discontinueds. If you're 60 or over, ask about their additional discount for seniors.

ADDRESS: 1727 N. 1st Street
San Jose
Map I No. 32

PHONE: (408) 298-4203

HOURS: Monday   8:30-5:30
Tuesday-Friday   8:30-9
Saturday and Sunday closed

PAYMENT: VISA, MasterCard, checks, and cash

RETURNS: They honor factory warranties, repairing or replacing at their option. They're very interested in pleasing the customer, so expect satisfaction.

LAYAWAY: No

GOLD HANGER claims to have the largest selection of proportioned-to-fit women's pants in California. Personally, I'm not counting, but the selection is quite large. Look for sizes 6 to 20 and 32 to 46, all in varying lengths to fit just about anyone. To coordinate with all those pants, a full selection of tops and other women's apparel is available, too. In those items, they carry sizes 5 to 15, 6 to 18, and S, M, and L. Dressing rooms are comfortable and private.

Everything is first quality in all three local stores and service is excellent.

ADDRESS/ Hacienda Gardens Shopping Center
PHONE: San Jose
(408) 266-4653
Map N No. 33

San Tomas Plaza
Campbell
(408) 374-4653
Map M No. 33

Mervyn's Plaza
Santa Clara
(408) 248-4653
Map H No. 33

HOURS: Monday-Friday   10-9
Saturday   10-5:30
Sunday   12-5

PAYMENT: VISA, MasterCard, Gold Card, checks, and cash

RETURNS: With receipt, for refund, exchange or store credit; ask about time restrictions at time of purchase.

LAYAWAY: No, but they will hold items for you—ask.

THE GOOD BUY SHOP is

literally packed with misses and juniors clothing from Emporium-Capwell stores in the area. This is an outlet store for women's clothing that was not sold in the stores. They carry blouses, skirts, pants, dresses, coats, summer wear, suits, and more. You'll find the same excellent quality available in Emporium-Capwell stores, and the savings are tremendous. Many prices are below cost.

You won't find all styles in all sizes, but everyone, regardless of age, size, or style preference, will find something to her liking at the GOOD BUY SHOP. I recommend it highly. Merchandise moves and changes fast, so keep checking for more bargains.

ADDRESS: Almaden Plaza near Emporium-
Capwell
San Jose
Map N No. 34

PHONE: (408) 265-1111

HOURS: Monday-Friday   10-9
Saturday   10-6
Sunday   12-5

PAYMENT: Emporium-Capwell Charge, checks, and cash

RETURNS: No, all sales are final

LAYAWAY: No

GOODE'S SAMPLE SHOP

carries a complete line of women's clothing including slacks, blouses, dresses, suits, formals, jackets, furs, and jewelry. Most items are salesman's samples, but you'll also find a selection of consignment items in excellent condition. On salesman's samples, they mark prices down 20% to start, then continue to mark down until they reach 75% off, so expect some terrific buys on their large selection. Besides regular women's sizes 5 to 20, they also frequently carry women's sizes 40 to 44, and occasionally they have a number of items in broken sizes (like a large group of 5's or 7's). Watch for their frequent half-off sales for even better bargains.

ADDRESS: 1393 Lincoln Avenue
San Jose
Map S No. 35

PHONE: (408) 293-8776

HOURS: Tuesday-Friday   10-5:30
Saturday   10-5
Sunday and Monday closed

PAYMENT: VISA, MasterCard, Gold Card, checks, and cash

RETURNS: For store credit only on returnable items. Ask at time of purchase.

LAYAWAY: 10% down, flexible terms; no layaway on sale items

HALF OR LESS is the outlet for J.M. McDonald's and sells women's, men's, and children's clothing that wasn't sold in the stores. Look for the same quality found in McDonald's, at about 50% off the regular price. Most sizes are available. The store is huge and holds a very large selection, especially in men's and women's apparel. The curtains on the dressing room doors (which face the store) don't close all the way, so, considering the co-ed clientele and my personal modesty, I bring a safety pin to secure the curtain from the inside. The customer returns unwanted try-ons to the racks, so some merchandise is mixed up. If you're willing to put up with these minor inconveniences, you can get some really tremendous bargains on the good brand-name clothes. Don't forget your safety pin.

ADDRESS: 330 N. Capitol Avenue (*not* Capitol Expressway)
San Jose
Map V No. 36

PHONE: (408) 258-6818

HOURS: Monday-Friday   10-7
Saturday   10-5:30
Sunday   1-5

PAYMENT: VISA, MasterCard, checks, and cash

RETURNS: For refund, exchange, or store credit with receipt

LAYAWAY: No

HOPPER, INC. wholesales steel and

hardware supplies, welding supplies, and medical supplies at savings up to 50% off regular retail prices. They are pleased to pass these savings on to the public and require no minimum purchase. You can buy just one hammer and save a bundle.

ADDRESS: 2290 De La Cruz Boulevard
Santa Clara
Map I No. 37

PHONE: (408) 727-5900

HOURS: Monday-Friday   7:30-5
Saturday and Sunday closed

PAYMENT: VISA, MasterCard, checks, and cash

HOUSE OF BEDSPREADS is

a shining star in bargain hunter's paradise. Here you'll find over 3000 absolutely first quality bedspreads, draperies to match, all kinds of pillows, comforters, snug sacs, a superior line of brass beds, and much more. The quality of all merchandise is strictly tops and discounts range from

20% to 40% off regular retail—sometimes more. If you don't find precisely what you're looking for, you may furnish the fabric and House of Bedspreads will have it made and, if you like, quilted—again, at a large discount. They carry exquisite quilted satin bedspreads and brass beds you would die for. Do yourself a favor and check it out.

ADDRESS/ PHONE: 417 Town and Country Village
San Jose
(408) 244-2148
Map H No. 38

Robertsville Square
5021 Almaden Expressway
San Jose
(408) 267-9950
Map N No. 38

HOURS: Monday-Saturday   10-6
Thursday   til 9
Sunday   12-5

PAYMENT: VISA, MasterCard, checks, and cash

RETURNS: Ask at time of purchase

LAYAWAY: No

HUN-I-NUT COMPANY

carries a varied and interesting inventory of imported foods from Middle Eastern, Balkan, and European countries. Though they sell mainly to stores and restaurants, they're pleased to sell direct to the public at low wholesale prices, in many cases 20% to 25% off regular retail. This is a fun place to shop if you're adventurous and like to try new and different foods.

ADDRESS: 795 The Alameda
San Jose
Map J No. 39

PHONE: (408) 286-8202

HOURS: Monday-Friday   10-5
Saturday   11-3
Sunday   closed

PAYMENT: Cash only

JAMBOREE offers first quality, name brand children's apparel at discounts of 20% to 50% off regular retail prices. In sizes infant through 14 in boys' and girls' clothing, Jamboree carries overruns, closeouts, discontinueds, and last season's styles (no irregulars or seconds) at prices from 99¢ to $50. Some of the fine lines available here are Rob Roy, Levi's, Pierre Cardin, Jack Tar, Marshall Sinclair, Yves St. Laurent, Dittos, and Pacific Trail. The store is carpeted and decorated, and all merchandise is well-displayed and arranged for ease of selection. You'll find some very stylish items here, including boys' suits, pants, shirts, pajamas, and jackets; for girls, they have dresses, sunsuits, jackets, skirts, blouses, pants, etc.

ADDRESS: 1649 Hollenbeck Avenue
Loehmann's Plaza
Sunnyvale
Map E No. 40

PHONE: (408) 739-3337

HOURS: Monday-Saturday   9:30-6
Wednesday   til 9:30
Sunday   12-5

PAYMENT: VISA, MasterCard, checks, and cash

RETURNS: With receipt, for store credit, exchange, or credit on a charge purchase, except on marked-down items which are not returnable

LAYAWAY: No

JAN'S BODY SHOPPE carries

first quality, very stylish women's fashions in sizes 3 to 20 and men's shirts in S, M, and L. The store is nicely carpeted and has private dressing rooms and music. There are a few children's selections but most are ladies'. All merchandise is overruns (no irregulars) at 30% to 70% off regular retail prices. They also carry belts, jewelry, and T-shirts with iron-on decal equipment and a large selection of decals to choose from. I am very pleased to have found two lovely blouses for myself at excellent prices and recommend checking out this store, particularly if you're a young woman or a T-shirt freak.

ADDRESS: 76 S. Park Victoria
Milpitas
Map R No. 41

PHONE: (408) 263-7722

HOURS: Monday and
 Saturday   10-5
Tuesday-Friday   10-8
Sunday   12-5

PAYMENT: VISA, MasterCard, checks, and cash

RETURNS: No, all sales are final

LAYAWAY: Minimum $2 down, pickup in 30 days

JOHNSON BROTHERS DISTRIBUTING is a wholesale dis-

tributor of cheeses and some meats that will sell direct to the public in minimum purchases of $100. You must order ahead, so call and find out what their range of products is. For savings of at least 20% to 30% off regular retail on these perishables, it would definitely pay to start a food buying co-op or, if necessary, just get together with friends and neighbors to make these minimum purchases.

ADDRESS: 66 Bonaventura Drive
San Jose
Map G No. 42

PHONE: (408) 263-4417

HOURS: Monday-Thursday   7-3
Friday   7-noon
Saturday and Sunday closed

PAYMENT: Checks and cash

KEDDIE KREATIONS is a

designer and manufacturer of ladies' sportswear and some children's clothes. Their main focus is on ladies' tennis clothes, warmups, and running suits, but you will also find separates (skirts, blouses, and shorts) and dresses, all in sizes 6 through 14 (sometimes 16's and 18's, too). Children's clothes run from sizes 2T through 8. You can buy direct from this manufacturer and save 35% to 75% off the regular retail prices. In some cases, this is less than wholesale.

ADDRESS: 99 Notre Dame Avenue
San Jose
Map J No. 44

PHONE: (408) 293-7639

HOURS: Monday-Friday   7-3:30
Saturday and Sunday closed

PAYMENT: Checks and cash

RETURNS: No, all sales are final

LAYAWAY: No

LAWRENCE CONTRACT FURNISHERS,
in business for 21 years, offers wallpaper and draperies at 30% off, fine furniture at 33% off, and carpeting and vinyl at 15% to 50% off regular retail prices. Lines they carry are Bigelow, Custom Weave, Calloway, Mohawk, Bassett, and many, many others. All their first quality merchandise is displayed in a large, well-kept showroom. One of their best offerings is discontinued carpeting.

ADDRESS: 470 Vandell Way
Campbell
Map L No. 45

PHONE: (408) 374-7590

HOURS: Monday-Friday   8:30-5:30
Saturday and Sunday closed

PAYMENT: Checks, cash, and financing
available

RETURNS: Only when previously undetected manufacturers' damage is found, otherwise, no

LAYAWAY: 1/3 down, terms flexible

LESTER BROTHERS is a farm

about a quarter mile south of Coyote on Monterey Road between San Jose and Morgan Hill that sells direct to you at 30% to 50% off prices in grocery stores (and many roadside stands). They grow and sell walnuts, dried apricots, dried prunes, and fresh cherries. They also sell fireplace wood at competitive prices. These friendly people are happy to help you save $$. When you get there, drive into the yard and toot your horn, and one of the family will come out to greet you.

ADDRESS: Corner of Montery Road and
Bailey Avenue
Map U No. 46

PHONE: (408) 227-6507

HOURS: Monday-Saturday   8-5
Sunday   closed

PAYMENT: Checks and cash

LINDA VISTA FOODS is a food

wholesaler that normally sells to markets, schools, and restaurants, but is pleased to offer dented cans and odd lots to the public at sizable savings, normally 20% to 40% off regular supermarket prices. You must order by phone at present and buy in minimums of one-case lots, so call ahead for prices and to find out what they have available.

ADDRESS: 750 N. 9th Street
San Jose
Map J No. 47

PHONE: (408) 297-3521

HOURS: Monday-Friday   8-5
Saturday and Sunday closed

PAYMENT: Checks and cash

RETURNS: Ask at time of purchase

LINEN FACTORY OUTLET

is an outlet store for a manufacturer of fine quality table linens (place mats, matching napkins, table cloths, runners, etc.), kitchen linens (pot holders, towels, appliance covers), aprons (including dressy aprons and a good selection of aprons with humorous sayings and illustrations), and other hostess apparel. Also offered are mandarin jackets and casual and hostess skirts in missy sizes 8 to 18. All fabrics are permanent press and workmanship is excellent. This fine merchandise is available for 40% to 70% off the prices it is sold for in the stores which buy from this manufacturer.

ADDRESS: 2200 Zanker Road, Suite D
San Jose
Map G No. 48

PHONE: (408) 263-8300

HOURS: Monday-Friday   8-4
Saturday   10-4
Sunday   closed

PAYMENT: VISA, MasterCard, checks, and cash

RETURNS: No, all sales are final

LAYAWAY: No

LOEHMANN'S is famous for its
original New York store which offered high-
fashion women's apparel at a discount before
anyone else. Now there are many stores
throughout the United States, and we're very
fortunate to have one in the South Bay Area.
Loehmann's specializes in designer, high-fashion,
high-quality clothing at discounts of at least 30%
off regular retail prices and sometimes much
more. Expect to find labels cut out (which is a
good sign) of silk, wool, cotton and other finely
styled and manufactured apparel. You'll find
dresses, skirts, blouses, suits, scarves, handbags,
blazers, slacks, jeans, hats, belts, coats, and more.
The selection is large, as are the community
dressing rooms. Sizes are 3-15 and 4-20. To keep
the overhead down, there are no assistants on
the floor to help you with your selections, and
there are no carpets or other amenities, which,
of course, reflects in your savings.

ADDRESS: 1651 Hollenbeck Avenue
Loehmann's Plaza
Sunnyvale
Map E No. 49

PHONE: (408) 737-1900

HOURS: Monday-Saturday   10-5:30
Wednesday   til 9:30
Sunday   closed

PAYMENT: Cash and checks only

RETURNS: No, all sales are final

LAYAWAY: No, but you can put 1/3 down,
and they'll hold it for you for one
week.

THE LUGGAGE CLEARANCE CENTER is an

outlet for a local luggage retail store offering all first quality luggage at 25% to 65% off regular retail. Familiar brand names available here are Samsonite, Skyway, American Tourister, and Lark. Selections are large and ever-changing, so, if you're looking for a particular item, keep checking. You never know when it may show up. Also, check their inventory of attache cases, wallets, and handbags. The Center is located near the airport, in case you're in a hurry to get out of town.

ADDRESS: 780 Coleman
San Jose
Map I No. 50

PHONE: (408) 294-4779

HOURS: Monday-Friday   10-6
Saturday   10-5
Sunday   12-5

PAYMENT: VISA, MasterCard, checks, and cash

RETURNS: For refund or exchange

MACY'S CLEARANCE CENTER houses Macy's discontinued

items, floor samples, special purchases, and dead-end merchandise—everything you would find in Macy's, including furniture, lamps, appliances, rugs, televisions, stereos, radios, mirrors, clocks, clothing and much, much more. Discounts of 20% to 50% are normal in this huge (40,000 square foot) building. One of their best deals is on linens—sheets, towels, etc. There is a minimal charge for deliveries.

ADDRESS: 5160 Stevens Creek Boulevard
(corner of Lawrence Expressway)
San Jose
Map F No. 51

PHONE: (408) 248-6343

HOURS: Monday-Friday   10-9
Saturday   9:30-6
Sunday   12-5

PAYMENT: Macy's Charge, American Express,
checks, and cash

RETURNS: No, all sales are final

LAYAWAY: No

MANUFACTURER'S CLOTHING OUTLET

(MCO) has become one of my favorite places to shop for work and sportswear. At 50% to 70% off regular retail (and sometimes more on sale and clearance items), you will find many well-known, first quality lines, including some "designer" lines. MCO carries overruns, samples, and a few irregulars for men, women, and children, and they receive frequent shipments of new merchandise. The selection is large and ever-changing. For women in sizes 4 to 20, 32 to 42, and 3/4 to 15/16, look for skirts, pants, blouses, jackets, sweaters, and suits. In sizes S, M, L, and XL and all regular men's sizes, they carry a fine selection of slacks, shirts, overcoats, sports jackets, ski jackets, and more. At special request, big and tall men's sizes are available to order in corduroy and wool sports jackets. In children's sizes 4 to 20, you will find jeans, cords, shirts, tops, down vests and jackets, and underwear. A friendly and efficient staff is on hand to assist you.

ADDRESS: 675 E. Brokaw Road
San Jose
Map G No. 52

PHONE: (408) 279-3855

HOURS: Monday-Saturday 10-6
Thursday and Friday til 7
Sunday 12-5

PAYMENT: MasterCard, VISA, checks, and cash

RETURNS: For exchange only if returned with receipt within two weeks of purchase, except sale items which are final sale

LAYAWAY: 50% down and pickup in 30 days

MANUFACTURER'S OUTLET STORE (MOS) offers

good service, a lovely decor with carpeting and music, and fine quality, brand name fashions for the mature and working woman. These over-runs, close-outs, discontinueds, and some irregulars come in sizes 6-18 and 5-15 in lines such as Koret, Act III, Fire Islander, RRRuss, Koko Knit, Byer, Shapely, and more. In addition to the fine selection of dresses, blouses, sweaters, jackets, and slacks, they also carry accessories such as belts, scarves, and handbags, all at approximately 20% off regular retail.

ADDRESS: 344 California Street
Palo Alto
Map A No. 53

PHONE: (415) 321-4385

HOURS: Monday-Saturday 10-5:30
Sunday closed

PAYMENT: VISA, MasterCard, checks, and cash

RETURNS: With receipt, merchandise can be returned for store credit or refund, except sale items which are final sale.

LAYAWAY: 20% down, monthly payments

MARSHALL'S...

If you haven't already discovered Marshall's, you're in for a delightful surprise. Marshall's carries a huge selection (in a huge store) of ladies', children's, and men's clothing, beddings, domestics, giftware, shoes and boots, linens, rugs, skiwear, coats, purses, and much more. Most merchandise is first quality overruns, samples, or stock manufactured expressly for Marshall's, with a limited selection of irregulars with minor flaws (all marked, of course). They carry many good quality (and some designer) lines including Pierre Cardin, Gant, Elles Belles, Ellen Tracy, Teddy, Diane Von Furstenberg, White Stag, Gloria Vanderbilt, Tami, Sassoon, Levi's, Fritzi, and many, many more. Women's apparel comes in sizes up to 50, and the selection is enormous in all types of clothing. Men's clothing sizes vary, but you will normally find up to size 50. Children's sizes include infant, toddler, and 4 to 14. Considering the 20% to 60% savings (and sometimes more on sale items) and the selection offered here, this is one place everyone needs to shop.

ADDRESS/ 5160 Stevens Creek Boulevard
PHONE: San Jose
(408) 244-8962
Map F No. 54

2845 Meridian (Hacienda Gardens
Shopping Center)
San Jose
(408) 267-0922
Map N No. 54

HOURS: Monday-Saturday   9:30-9:30
Sunday   12-5

PAYMENT: VISA, MasterCard, checks, and cash

RETURNS: Refunds within 14 days of
purchase with receipt; after 14
days, store exchange or store
credit only with receipt

LAYAWAY: 10% down and pickup in 30 days

THE MART is one of a chain of stores
selling office furniture and accessories at
substantial discounts. Their inventory includes
desks, chairs, file cabinets, lamps, and chair mats.
Most pieces are first quality, but the few slightly
damaged items are discounted even further.
Compare their prices on this brand name furniture and you'll be pleasantly surprised.

ADDRESS: 2010 Duane Avenue
Santa Clara
Map G No. 55

PHONE: (408) 727-4246

HOURS: Monday-Friday   8:30-5:30
Saturday   10-4
Sunday   closed

PAYMENT: VISA, MasterCard, Gold Card,
checks, and cash

RETURNS: Ask at time of purchase.

LAYAWAY: 10% down, time negotiable

M. JESSUP SALVAGE is like a

large surplus store, specializing in damaged freight, train salvage, overruns from gift shows, and liquidations, and that includes all kinds of merchandise. Some of the things I found at 40% (and more) off regular retail prices were: non-perishable foods, clothing, books, wigs, office supplies, sundries, glassware, frames, shoes, rugs, sewing supplies, garden supplies, candles, toys, and auto supplies. Merchandise changes all the time with shipments coming in two or three times a week, so best to check often if you're a real bargain shopper.

ADDRESS: 705 N. 13th Street
San Jose
Map J No. 57

PHONE: (408) 295-8696

HOURS: Tuesday-Saturday   10-6
Sunday   12-5
Monday   closed

PAYMENT: VISA, MasterCard, checks, and cash

RETURNS: With receipt and tags for refund, store credit, or exchange

LAYAWAY: No

MPM, INC. specializes in office furni-

ture at wholesale prices. Well known in the area for their discount prices on all types of office furniture, they carry desks, chairs, cabinets, and bookcases, among other things. Everything is factory direct.

ADDRESS: 180 E. Sunnyoaks
Campbell
Map L No. 58

PHONE: (408) 379-9751

HOURS: Tuesday-Saturday   9-5
Sunday and Monday closed

PAYMENT: VISA, MasterCard, checks, and cash

RETURNS: For cash refund or exchange

LAYAWAY: No

MR. MEAT is a real old-fashioned
butcher shop offering excellent service and up to
40% off regular retail prices. If meat takes the
biggest chunk out of your food budget (as it does
for most of us), Mr. Meat can't be beat. The
butchers are pleased to tell you what the best
buys are and how to select certain cuts, and they
will cut to your order. They have top quality
USDA Choice meat, poultry, and seafood, some
deli items and a few standard grocery items.
Since they buy straight from the meat packers,
thereby eliminating the middle man, they can
pass the savings on to you while still offering the
very best service.

ADDRESS/ 1745 Berryessa Road
PHONE: San Jose
(408) 923-8244
Map V No. 59

1720 Park Avenue
San Jose
(408) 998-8558
Map I No. 59

HOURS:	Monday-Friday	10-7
	Saturday	9-6
	Sunday	closed

PAYMENT: VISA, MasterCard, Food Stamps, checks, and cash

RETURNS: For refund or exchange

NETO SAUSAGE COMPANY
is a wholesaler which sells to other stores and also to the public. The store in front of the plant offers sausages, cheeses, fish, canned imports, wines, and more for 35% to 45% off regular retail prices. No minimum purchase is required, but they do offer additional discounts on purchases in quantity. For parties, group gatherings, or just for your family's needs, this in one of the best places around to save money on food.

ADDRESS: 3499 The Alameda
Santa Clara
Map I No. 60

PHONE: (408) 296-0818

HOURS:	Monday-Saturday	7-5
	Friday	7-6
	Sunday	closed

PAYMENT: Cash and Food Stamps

THE NORTHSIDE WALNUT SHELLING COMPANY,
in business since 1951, does just what its name suggests—shells walnuts!

And, lucky for us, they sell them to the public at wholesale prices. At last check, they were selling shelled walnuts for $2 per pound in 5-pound minimum purchases. They also handle almonds at similar savings. Most of their sales are to the large supermarkets under a very familiar label. Though their processing is done October through March, they're open all year round for all you wal-nuts.

ADDRESS: 590 N. 5th Street at Jackson
San Jose
Map J No. 61

PHONE: (408) 294-0336

HOURS: Monday-Friday   7-3:30
Saturday and Sunday closed

PAYMENT: Cash only

RETURNS: For cash refund or exchange

OLD WORLD CHEESE COMPANY

is a distributor and whole-saler of cheeses, cold meats, pastas, peanut butter, olive oil, and more. They sell mostly to groups and co-ops, but individuals are shopping there more often as grocery store prices rise. Small minimum purchases are required, but with 30% to 50% off grocery store prices, who's complaining? Except for hot dogs, which are sold in 10-pound packages, minimums are generally 3 pounds for each item. Merchandise turns over fast so is very fresh. Call for information on group and co-op orders.

ADDRESS: 932 EL Camino
Sunnyvale
Map D No. 62

PHONE: (408) 737-1854

HOURS: Monday-Saturday   10-6
Sunday   closed

PAYMENT: Checks, cash, and Food Stamps

OROWEAT BAKERY OUTLET
sells all the fine Oroweat products at up to 50% off regular retail prices. Stock up on bread, buns, rolls, cookies, pastries, croutons, and bread sticks at these great savings. Look for extra special bargains on week-old baked goods.

ADDRESS: 456 W. Maude
Sunnyvale
Map C No. 63

PHONE: (408) 732-0382

HOURS: Monday, Tuesday,
    Thursday, Friday   9-5:30
Wednesday   9:30-5:30
Saturday   9:30-5
Sunday   closed

PAYMENT: Checks, cash, and Food Stamps

PAPER FACTORY STORE
offers complete wedding and anniversary papers and accessories; supplies for banquets, parties, and holidays; stationery; wrapping papers; ribbons; yarns; shelf paper; school supplies; office supplies; and lots more. Everything is first quality, except for paper towels and bathroom tissue, which are seconds (who cares?). Normal savings are up to 40% off regular retail prices, with sub-

stantial additional discounts for volume purchases. Printing is available for book matches, napkins, invitations, stationery, etc. They have a lot of experience with wedding papers, and their prices in that area are practically unbeatable.

ADDRESS/ 1400 Kifer Road
PHONE: Sunnyvale
(408) 739-8070
Map Q No. 64

827 W. Hamilton
Campbell
(408) 379-5940
Map M No. 64

HOURS: Monday-Friday   9-4:30
Saturday   9-3:30
Sunday   closed

PAYMENT: VISA, MasterCard, checks, and cash

RETURNS: For exchange or store credit

PARISIAN BAKERIES THRIFT STORE
is an outlet for all the fine baked goods produced by Parisian Bakeries. They offer very good discounts on all their products, many of which are fresh from the bakery (which is in the same building). Other items are over-bakes and second day goods. Best days to shop here for the bargains are Monday and Thursday.

ADDRESS: 1854 S. 7th Street
San Jose
Map K No. 65

PHONE: (408) 293-3040

HOURS: Monday-Saturday   9-5:30
(closed from noon
   to 1 on Tuesday
   and Wednesday)
Sunday   closed

PAYMENT: Cash and Food Stamps

PATTY QUINN'S is one of my

favorite stores for designer fashions at some
terrific prices. Though their normal discounts are
30% to 60% off regular retail, I have personally
saved as much as 75% on sale items. Some of the
well-known lines you'll find in Patty Quinn's are
Calvin Klein, Anne Klein, Gloria Vanderbilt, Evan
Picone, Modern Juniors, Koret, Adolfo, Misty
Harbor, and more. They also carry other high
quality lines from the East Coast that are generally unfamiliar to California buyers. You can
try it all on in private dressing rooms with lots
of mirrors. Most items are first quality overruns,
samples, closeouts, and discontinueds, but they
do carry just a few irregulars. All ladies' clothes
are in sizes 4 to 18. In the limited, but fashionable, men's department, sizes are S, M, L, and XL
and pants sizes. The store is carpeted and large
and merchandise is well-displayed.

ADDRESS: 1585 N. 4th Street
San Jose
Map J No. 66

PHONE: (408) 288-9179

HOURS: Monday-Saturday   10-6
Thursday   til 9
Sunday   12-5

PAYMENT: VISA, MasterCard, checks, and cash

RETURNS: For store credit or exchanges only with receipt, except for sale items which are final sale

LAYAWAY: 50% down and pickup in 30 days

PIC 'N SAVE, one of a chain of 73, is a huge store packed full of an exciting and ever-changing selection of all new merchandise, mostly first quality with some irregulars and seconds. Truckloads of new merchandise come in weekly and stock turns around fast. Everything is acquired from liquidated businesses and is offered at 40% to 70% off regular retail prices. Some of the things I found when I went were men's, women's , and children's clothing (all kinds); housewares; bedding; kitchen linens; shoes; cosmetics; lots of toys; office supplies; books; arts and crafts supplies; stationery; non-perishable food items; purses; sporting equipment; dishes; rugs; framed prints; pots and pans; plastic-ware; hardware; gardening supplies; pet supplies; baskets (all kinds and sizes); artificial flowers; candles; light bulbs; bric-a-brac; chairs; jewelry; and much, much more. You never know what you'll find here, so this is really a fun place to explore.

ADDRESS: 75 N. Weller
Milpitas
Map R No. 67

PHONE: (408) 262-9967

HOURS: Monday-Saturday   9-9
Sunday   10-7

PAYMENT: Cash and checks only

RETURNS: For refund or store exchange with receipt only

PINKY'S FASHIONS has two

locations to serve us with women's clothing and
accessories at 20% to 50% off regular retail
prices. Savings are sometimes greater on sale
items. They stock very nice fashions, all first
quality and direct from the manufacturer. Sizes
range from 3 to 20 in quality lines such as Bobbie Brooks, Byer, Wrangler, Devon, and more.

ADDRESS/ 1409 Bird Avenue
PHONE: Willow Glen area of San Jose
(408) 286-8181
Map S No. 68

1049 Capitol Expressway
Gould Shopping Center
San Jose
(408) 629-3880
Map T No. 68

HOURS: Monday-Friday   10-6
Saturday   10-5
Sunday   closed

PAYMENT: VISA, MasterCard, Gold Card,
checks, and cash

RETURNS: Ask at time of purchase

LAYAWAY: 10% down and pickup in 30 days

PISANO THRIFT STORE

wholesales Pisano's own brand of french breads
and some fresh pastries. There's a small deli
here, too, serving sandwiches and such. Discounts on bakery items are approximately 25%
off regular retail and sometimes greater.

ADDRESS: 1551 Parkmoor Street
San Jose
Map I No. 69

PHONE: (408) 998-1166

HOURS: Monday-Saturday   8:45-5:15
Sunday   closed

PAYMENT: Checks, cash, and Food Stamps

POND PRODUCTS COMPANY is a distributor of high-quality natural foods. They sell to health food and grocery stores and to the public in minimums of one-case lots at wholesale prices. Some of their offerings are honey, preserves and marmalade, dressings, cookies, crackers, dried fruit, healthful candy (carob balls, fruit rolls, etc.), teas, nuts and seeds, cereals, pasta, and trail mixes ("nutty buddies"). Call for ordering information, pickup details, and a list of available products and prices.

ADDRESS: 1360 White Oaks Avenue
Campbell
Map L No. 70

PHONE: (408) 377-2082

HOURS: Monday-Friday   9-5
Saturday   9-12
Sunday   closed

PAYMENT: Checks and cash

POTTERY SALES, INC.

wholesales nursery pottery for 20% to 50% off the regular retail prices. In their small showroom, they display a large selection of closeouts, seconds, and discontinued hand-thrown stoneware.

ADDRESS: 490 Howard
San Jose
Map J No. 71

PHONE: (408) 295-9522

HOURS: Monday-Saturday   9-5
Sunday   closed

PAYMENT: VISA, MasterCard, checks, and cash

RETURNS: With receipt, for cash refund or store exchange

RAGSMATAZZ is one of a chain of 9

stores specializing in junior women's pants, dresses, jackets, sweaters, t-shirts, blazers, skirts, and suits. (They're sold in separate pieces for all you ladies with one skirt size and a different jacket size—voila!) You'll find all these brand-name and stylish fashions at 30% to 50% off regular retail in sizes 1 to 13 and S, M, L. Many of the labels are cut out here, which is a good sign of quality (though not the only criterion, of course).

ADDRESS: Village Corners Shopping Center
(in the inner mall)
Corner of San Antonio Road and El
Camino
Los Altos
Map B No. 72

PHONE: (415) 941-2792

HOURS: Monday-Saturday   10-6
Sunday   11-5

PAYMENT: VISA, MasterCard, checks, and cash

RETURNS: With receipt, for exchange or store credit within 7 days of purchase

LAYAWAY: No, but they will hold an article up to 3 days

REMNANT WORLD specializes in

carpet remnants selling at 40% off regular retail. Most remnants are top quality, but the few seconds are marked down accordingly. They will install, or you can save even more and install it yourself with their instructions.

ADDRESS: 5160 Stevens Creek Boulevard
San Jose
Map F No. 73

PHONE: (408) 984-1965

HOURS: Monday-Friday   10-9
Saturday   9-6
Sunday   12-5

PAYMENT: VISA, MasterCard, Gold Card, checks, and cash

RETURNS: For refund or exchange

LAYAWAY: No, but they will hold remnants for a reasonable (negotiable) length of time.

ROCKWELL sells new and reconditioned hand power tools at savings up to 40% off regular retail prices. They carry drills, sanders, saws, routers, hammers, grinders, and more. Warranties apply but are limited depending on the item purchased. Ask for details at time of purchase.

ADDRESS: 2305 De La Cruz Boulevard
Santa Clara
Map I No. 74

PHONE: (408) 727-9790

HOURS: Monday-Friday   8-5
Saturday   9-1
Sunday   closed

PAYMENT: VISA, MasterCard, checks, and cash

RETURNS: Warranties are honored

ROMA BAKERY is a landmark bakery in San Jose. This family-owned enterprise has been in business for 75 years baking their wonderful french bread and rolls. Though they sell mainly to restaurants all over California, you can buy minimums of 5 each of loaves of bread or dozens of rolls at wholesale prices.

ADDRESS: 655 Almaden Avenue
San Jose
Map J No. 75

PHONE: (408) 294-0123

HOURS: Monday, Tuesday, Thursday,
Friday, Saturday   8-5
Wednesday and Sunday   closed

PAYMENT: Checks and cash

ROYAL BEAUTY SUPPLY

offers brand name cosmetics and beauty supplies at 20% to 33% off regular retail prices, and these discounts are not just for the professionals. Of the 5 stores in this chain, the San Jose store is the only one selling direct to the public. Here you'll find your favorites in Revlon, Wella, Faberge, Clairol, Palm Beach, and more. Royal buys direct from the manufacturers, so they can offer you these excellent products at substantial savings.

ADDRESS: 3455 Stevens Creek Boulvard
San Jose
Map H No. 76

PHONE: (408) 248-4072

HOURS: Monday-Friday   8-5
Saturday   8-noon
Sunday   closed

PAYMENT: Checks and cash

RETURNS: Some items are returnable for refund or exchange. Ask at time of purchase.

SCOTTY MAC'S wholesales first

quality carpeting at 20% to 50% off regular retail. Their excellent prices also include padding and installation.

ADDRESS: 538 Trimble Road
San Jose
Map G No. 77

PHONE: (Not listed)

HOURS: Monday-Friday   9-9
Saturday   10-6
Sunday   12-5

PAYMENT: VISA, MasterCard, Gold Card, checks, and cash

S & G DISCOUNTS sells a large

selection of floor coverings and carpeting at between 30% and 70% off regular retail prices. All merchandise is first quality. Take your floor measurements along.

ADDRESS: 505 S. Market Street
San Jose
Map J No. 78

PHONE: (408) 292-4182

HOURS: Monday-Friday   9-6
Saturday   9-5
Sunday   closed

PAYMENT: VISA, MasterCard, Gold Card, checks, and cash

RETURNS: Ask at time of purchase

LAYAWAY: 10% down, terms negotiable

SHOE CITY, U.S.A. sells shoes for

the whole family at 33% to 80% off regular retail prices. Here you'll find such brands as Famolare, Garber, Joyce, Nina, Oscar De La Renta, Life Stride, Connies, Bare Traps, Amalfi, Cobbies, Pappagallo, AirStep, Nunn Bush and more in women's sizes 4 to 11, men's sizes 6 to 15, and children's sizes 3½ to 6. They offer a wide and attractive selection and have cut overhead to the bone to sell to you at these good savings. All merchandise is first quality overruns, closeouts, and discontinued styles purchased directly from the manufacturers. There are no exchanges or refunds, so make your selections carefully and enjoy!

ADDRESS: 1910 El Camino Real
Mountain View
Map B No. 79

PHONE: (415) 969-8393

HOURS: Monday-Saturday   9:30-6
Tuesday and
    Thursday   til 9
Sunday   closed

PAYMENT: Checks and cash only

RETURNS: No

LAYAWAY: 10% down and pickup within 30 days

SILVA SAUSAGE COMPANY is a manufacturer and

wholesaler of fine quality sausage selling mainly to supermarkets and restaurants but also direct to the public at the same wholesale prices. They make all kinds of sausages here (linguica, breakfast links, and chorizo, to name a few), which they sell in their factory store along with other delicatessen items (including sandwiches).

ADDRESS: 1266 E. Julian
San Jose
Map J No. 80

PHONE: (408) 293-5437

HOURS: Monday-Saturday   9-5
(Sandwiches are
  sold Monday-
  Friday from
  10-3:30)
Sunday   closed

PAYMENT: Checks and cash

SKIL POWER TOOL SERVICE CENTER
sells new, reconditioned power tools with full factory warranties at 40% to 60% off normal retail prices. They have saws, drills, sanders, hammers, screwdrivers, planers, routers, impact wrenches, grinders, polishers, and accessories. None of the merchandise is used, just found defective then reconditioned for sale at these great savings. You will also find some closeout items which are new (and don't require reconditioning) and also sold at a discount.

ADDRESS: 2130 De La Cruz Boulevard
Santa Clara
Map I No. 81

PHONE: (408) 727-9444

HOURS: Monday-Friday   8-5
Saturday and Sunday closed

PAYMENT: VISA, MasterCard, checks, and cash

RETURNS: Factory warranties are honored. In some cases, items can be returned for exchange or refund, which is negotiable. Also, there may be a 15% restocking fee depending on the circumstances. Ask for details at time of purchase.

SOMETHING SPECIAL is just

that...something special. This lovely store resembles a very special little boutique and carries high quality apparel at 20% to 80% off regular retail on overruns and closeouts (no irregulars). You will find up-to-the-minute styles in such lines as Plushbottoms, Ardee, Collage, Sticky Fingers, Larry Lavine, San Francisco Tea Party, Jonathan Martin, Shirt Strings, Sisley, and A. Smile, among others. They carry dresses, hats, pants, jeans, sweaters, and blouses, all in this season's styles, colors, and fabrics, and the selection is excellent. I recommend this store especially for young women, particularly of high school and college age.

ADDRESS/
PHONE: 255 University Avenue
Palo Alto
(415) 328-7361
Map A No. 82

19676 Stevens Creek Boulevard
Cupertino
(408) 446-2663
Map F No. 82

HOURS:

Monday-Friday	10-7
Thursday	til 8
Saturday	10-6
Sunday	12-5

PAYMENT: VISA, MasterCard, checks, and cash

RETURNS: Exchanges or store credit only with receipt

LAYAWAY: No

SPORTIQUE carries mostly women's apparel in sizes 3 to 20 (and some 1's and 2's) as well as a limited selection of men's and children's garments. Men's sizes are S, M, L, and XL, and available children's sizes are 4 to 10. They are known to carry over 300 lines of all first quality, brand name fashions. Now in the 9th year of business, Sportique is packed full of terrific clothes at prices bound to knock you out. Normal discounts are up to 60% off regular retail prices and, at one of their fantastic pre-season sales, you can save as much as 85%. (NOTE: This is one of the few discount stores that offers "pre-season" sales.) Some of the familiar lines carried here are Villager, Garland, Levi's, Fritzi, Time and Place, Chemin de Fer, EccoBay, Wrangler, Bobbie Brooks, Alex Colman, and many, many more. Sportique carries up-to-date styles and classics, too. I highly recommend getting on their mailing list, which announces their great sales.

ADDRESS: 2310 Homestead Road
Los Altos
Map E No. 83

PHONE: (415) 735-8660

HOURS: Monday-Friday   10-9
Saturday   10-6
Sunday   12-5

PAYMENT: VISA, MasterCard, checks, and cash

RETURNS: Refunds and bank charge credits within 10 days of purchase except on red-tag (clearance) items which are final sale. Exchanges and store credits within 21 days of purchase (except clearance items). All returns must be accompanied by the receipt. No returns on worn or washed garments.

LAYAWAY: 30% down and pickup in 21 days

STANDARD BEAUTY SUPPLY

is pleased to sell brand name cosmetics to the public (and to beauticians) at a discount. Both mother and daughter who work here are beauticians and thus are of great help in making selections. Everything is top quality and the selection is very good. Look for Jhermack, Wella, Clairol, Redken, and more.

ADDRESS: 1313 S. Winchester Boulevard
San Jose
Map M No. 84

PHONE: (408) 378-6840

HOURS:
Monday-Friday	10-6
Saturday	10-5
Sunday	closed

PAYMENT: VISA, MasterCard, checks, and cash

RETURNS: For store exchange unless irreplaceable, then for cash refund; ask at time of purchase.

STANDARD BRAND PAINTS,

in business since 1939, sells not only paint but also floor coverings, window treatments, wallpaper, carpeting, and all the tools and accessories you need to install all these things. Also look for art and hobby supplies, some hardware, a large selection of picture frames, roofing supplies, and lighting supplies. Best of all, everything is discounted 10% to 50%, and the service is better than in many regular retail stores of this type. The experienced and well-trained staff is available to assist you in making the appropriate selections and will be happy to give you countless tips on how to do the job once you get the materials home. Expect to become a regular at these fine stores. They meet the highest standards of good quality merchandise, good service, and discount prices. On items $10 or over, they offer an unconditional money-back guarantee. Returns on other items for exchange or store credit are handled swiftly and fairly.

ADDRESS/
PHONE: 456 Meridian
San Jose
(408) 292-8641
Map I No. 85

120 El Camino Real
Mountain View
(415) 965-1147
Map P No. 85

1020 Blossom Hill Road
San Jose
(408) 265-8076
Map N No. 85

HOURS: Monday-Friday   8-9
Saturday   8-6:30
Sunday   9-5:30

PAYMENT: VISA, MasterCard, checks, and cash

RETURNS: For refund or exchange with receipt

LAYAWAY: 10% down, pickup within 30 days

STANDARD FOOD WHOLESALERS

is a huge warehouse full of just about everything you'd find at a grocery store—and all at wholesale prices! Don't look for supermarket conveniences here, just great savings on everything. Specializing in all types of vending and catering foods, they carry everything but produce and meats (look through this book for other places to get those items). That includes brand name canned and packaged items, paper goods, laundry supplies, beverages, restaurant supplies, and much, much more. Service is minimal, as are the prices.

ADDRESS: 1130 N. 10th Street
San Jose
Map J No. 86

PHONE: (408) 275-1923 and 947-0300

HOURS: Monday-Friday   4:30AM-5PM
Saturday   8-noon
Sunday   closed

PAYMENT: Checks and cash

STEVENS CREEK SURPLUS

is a large, well-stocked surplus store carrying a wide variety of merchandise and an especially good selection of men's and women's pants and jeans. Among other things, they carry Levi's, shirts, thermal underwear, gloves, overalls, belts, socks, jackets, pants, and hats (for men, women, and children), plus work boots, sleeping bags, and sporting equipment. Markdown on Levi's is 10% to 20%, and the rest of the merchandise sells for 10% to 50% off regular retail. With a few exceptions, everything is first quality.

ADDRESS: 3449 Stevens Creek Boulevard
San Jose
Map H No. 87

PHONE: (408) 244-0773

HOURS: Monday-Friday   9-9
Saturday and Sunday 10-6

PAYMENT: VISA, MasterCard, Gold Card, checks, and cash

RETURNS: Refunds, exchange, or store credit within 15 days of purchase with a receipt, except sale items which can sometimes be exchanged or returned for store credit

LAYAWAY: 20% down and pickup in 30 days

STRATTON OF APTOS is a

manufacturer of fashionable (sometimes trend-setting), well-made designs by Kathy Stratton, the owner/designer. Her firm offers custom work and alterations in addition to her own line of dresses, blouses, pants, skirts, and suits. Some of her more original and creative designs are disco-type clothing in very contemporary colors and fabrics. In the small outlet store in front, you can get sizes 8 to 16 at 50% off the price they sell for in stores.

ADDRESS: 136 Kennedy Avenue
Campbell
Map L No. 88

PHONE: (408) 374-4376

HOURS: Monday-Friday   9-5
Saturday and Sunday closed

PAYMENT: Checks and cash only

RETURNS: For exchange or store credit only

LAYAWAY: Can be arranged

SUNBEAM APPLIANCE SERVICE COMPANY sells all
the small household appliances manufactured by
Sunbeam including hand mixers, can openers,
toasters, toaster ovens, irons, personal care
items, and more. Most items are factory reconditioned, but you will also find samples, closeouts, some new (that is, not requiring reconditioning), and seconds (mostly with cosmetic
blemishes not affecting the performance of the
product). Everything carries the same warranties
as a brand new item and is sold at least 15% to
25% off regular retail. In some cases, you'll pay
less than wholesale.

ADDRESS: 2100 De La Cruz Boulevard
Santa Clara
Map I No. 89

PHONE: (408) 727-6733

HOURS: Monday-Friday   8:30-5
Saturday and Sunday closed

PAYMENT: VISA, MasterCard, checks, and cash

RETURNS: Factory warranties are honored.
Ask for details at time of
purchase.

LAYAWAY: No

SUNNYVALE SHOE MART

carries over 50,000 pairs of name-brand shoes discounted an average of 25% (sometimes more). You will recognize such names as Famolare, Hush Puppies, AirStep, Naturalizer, and more. They carry a full line of ladies', children's, and men's shoes, including casual, work, dress and athletic shoes, and work and western boots. Friendly and helpful employees are available to assist you in trying on ladies' sizes 4-12, men's sizes 6-14, and children's sizes 4 and up.

ADDRESS: 1014 W. El Camino (at Mary)
Sunnyvale
Map D No. 90

PHONE: (408) 738-9836

HOURS: Monday-Friday 9-9
Saturday 9-6
Sunday 10-6

PAYMENT: VISA, MasterCard, Gold Card, checks, and cash

RETURNS: For store exchange or credit with receipt; no refunds

LAYAWAY: 10% down and 30-day pickup

TAGG'S

is a relatively new outlet for brand-name (and some designer) women's clothing at 20% to 60% off regular retail. They carry sizes 3 to 18 in pants, skirts, blouses, dresses, jackets, sportswear, etc. Everything is first quality and mostly geared toward the working woman, though you'll find a good variety and selection for most occasions. Dressing rooms are private, and merchandise is nicely displayed and organized.

ADDRESS/ 2932 Aborn Square
PHONE: Aborn Road and Capitol
Expressway
San Jose
(408) 274-9322
Map T No. 91

Hamilton Plaza Shopping Center
Hamilton and Bascom
Campbell
(408) 377-7544
Map M No. 91

Calaveras Plaza
Calaveras Road and Serra Road
Milpitas
(408) 262-0184
Map R No. 91

HOURS: Monday-Friday   10-9
Saturday   10-6
Sunday   12-5

PAYMENT: VISA, MasterCard, checks, and cash

RETURNS: With receipt for refund, exchange,
or store credit within 14 days of
purchase

LAYAWAY: 30% down, pickup in 30 days

TOSCANA BAKING COMPANY

sells baked goods at cost in this outlet store on Burke Street. Fresh items are sold at wholesale, and second-day items are sold at less than wholesale, so look for some really good savings here.

ADDRESS: 533 Burke Street
San Jose
Map K No. 92

PHONE: (408) 295-8435

HOURS: Monday-Thursday   8:30-1 and
                                                    1:30-5

Friday and Saturday 8:30-5
Sunday   closed

PAYMENT: Cash or Food Stamps

UNIVERSE PAINT CO. sells a
full line of all kinds of paint. While they sell
mostly to painting contractors, they are pleased
also to sell to the public. You can save $2 to $3
on each gallon purchased, and they will mix
whatever color you wish.

ADDRESS: 1639 Almaden Road
San Jose
Map S No. 93

PHONE: (408) 294-4344

HOURS: Monday-Friday   7-5:30
Saturday   8-4
Sunday   closed

PAYMENT: VISA, MasterCard, checks, and cash

WALLCOVERINGS
UNLIMITED carries all types of
wallcoverings, wall paints, and accessories at 20%
to 40% off regular retail prices. Everything is
first quality and in brand name lines. Besides the
quality and terrific savings here, they also offer
free classes in wallpapering.

ADDRESS: 2644 El Camino Real
Moonlite Shopping Center
Santa Clara
Map H No. 94

PHONE: (408) 247-4976

HOURS: Monday-Saturday   10-6
Friday   til 9
Sunday   12-4

PAYMENT: VISA, MasterCard, checks, and cash

RETURNS: For refund, exchange, or store credit

LAYAWAY: They will hold merchandise for
you for up to 30 days.

WAREHOUSE BEDROOMS

carries complete lines of bedroom furniture in
well-known brands at 20% to 50% off regular
retail prices. All merchandise is first quality and
carries full factory warranties. Some pieces have
been slightly damaged in freight and so are
marked down even further.

ADDRESS: 211 Weddell
Sunnyvale
Map C No. 95

PHONE: (408) 744-1701

HOURS: Monday-Friday   10-8
Thursday   10-6
Saturday   10-5
Sunday   12:30-5

PAYMENT: VISA, MasterCard, checks, and
cash. Financing is available.

RETURNS: Factory warranties are honored

LAYAWAY: 20% down, pickup within 60 days of purchase with payments due every two weeks. Terms are negotiable.

WESTERN CONTRACT FURNISHERS has been in business

for 25 years as a catalog store and showroom selling residential and office furniture. Merchandise on the showroom floor sells at manufacturer's list prices, which average about 30% off regular retail. However, at the twice-yearly sales, showroom merchandise is sold at a 40% discount. Catalog orders come in at 20% to 30% off regular retail, depending on the item purchased. Office furniture available is desks, chairs, and whole office-systems setups. Residential furnishings include brand name furniture, carpeting (at *very* competitive prices—among the best in the Bay Area), wallpaper, upholstery and drapery fabrics, and more.

ADDRESS: 175 Stockton
San Jose
Map I No. 96

PHONE: (408) 275-9600

HOURS: Monday-Friday   8:30-5:30
Saturday   10-5
Sunday   closed

PAYMENT: VISA, MasterCard, checks, and cash

RETURNS: Factory warranties are honored

LAYAWAY: No

WONDER—HOSTESS BAKERY THRIFT STORE

sells Hostess and Wonder Bread products at 30% off regular store prices. Wednesday is Bargain Day here, and senior citizens always get an additional 10% off. The store is very well kept and goodies are neatly displayed. If you're a Twinkie freak, this is the place to shop and save. Also look for muffins, fruit pies, buns, donuts, snack cakes, and all types of bread.

ADDRESS: 2450 De La Cruz Boulevard
Santa Clara
Map I No. 97

PHONE: (408) 727-5300

HOURS: Monday-Friday   9-5:30
Saturday   8:30-5
Sunday   11-4

PAYMENT: Checks, cash, and Food Stamps

MAPS

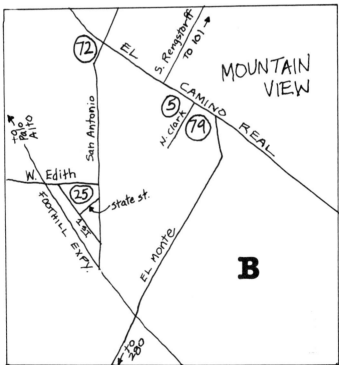

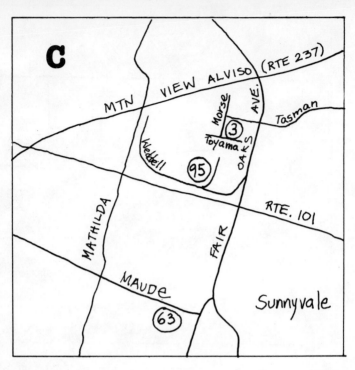

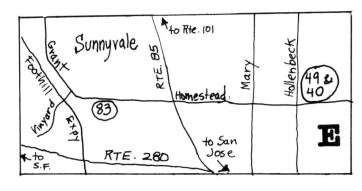

95

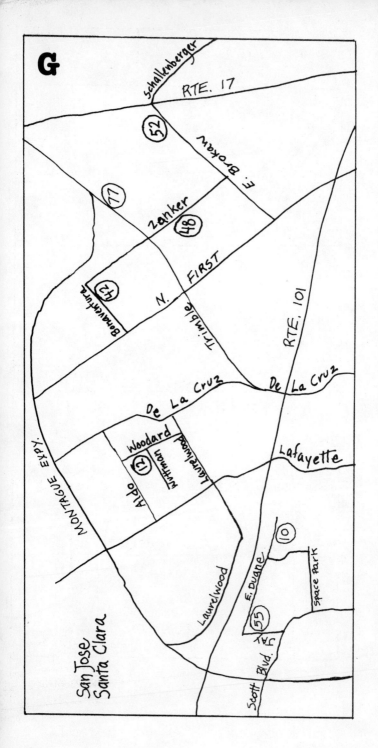

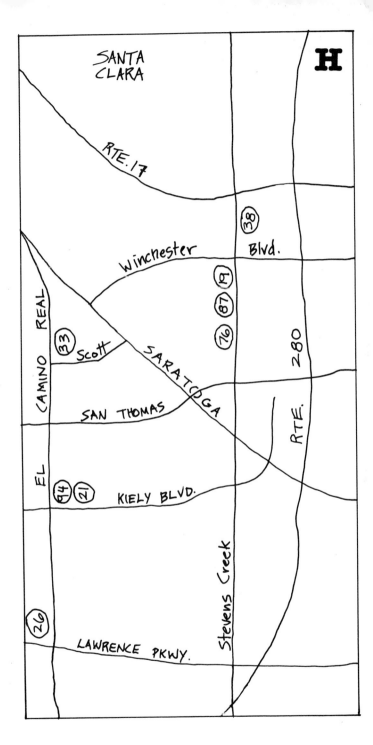

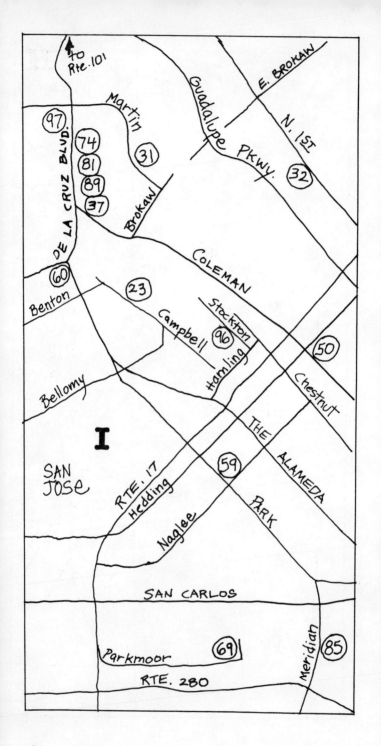

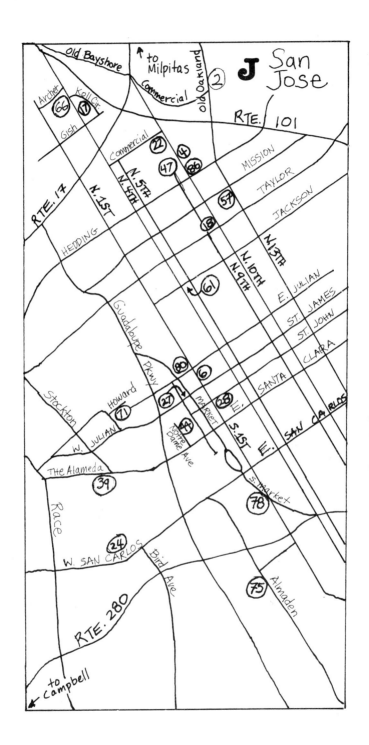

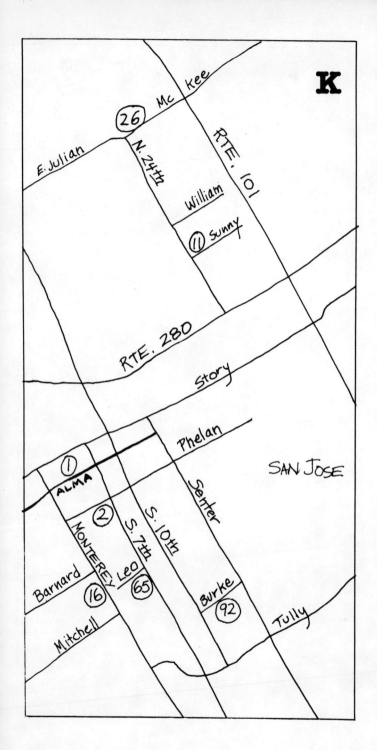

K

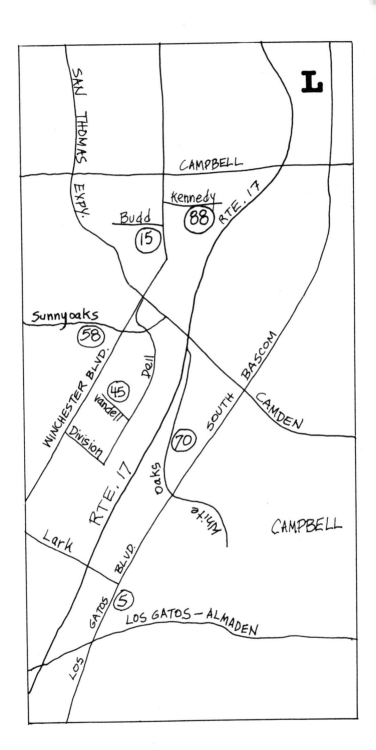

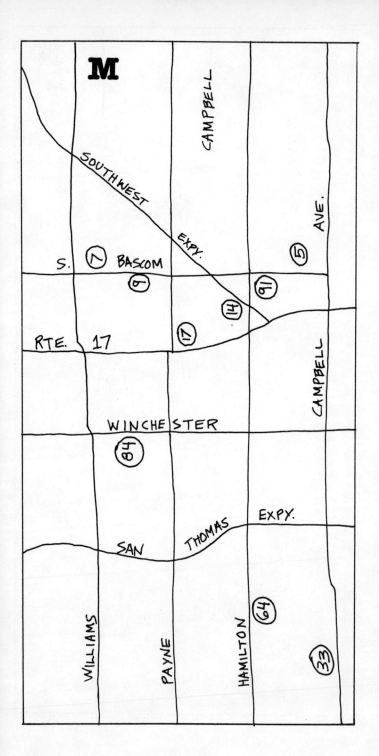

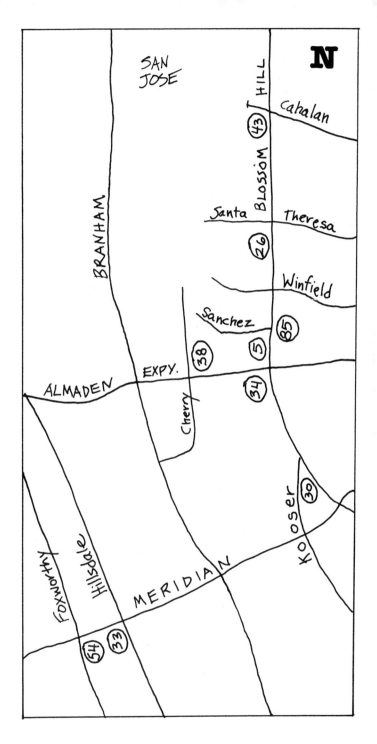

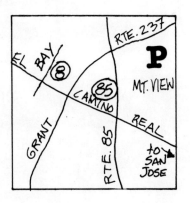

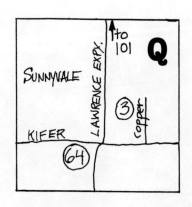

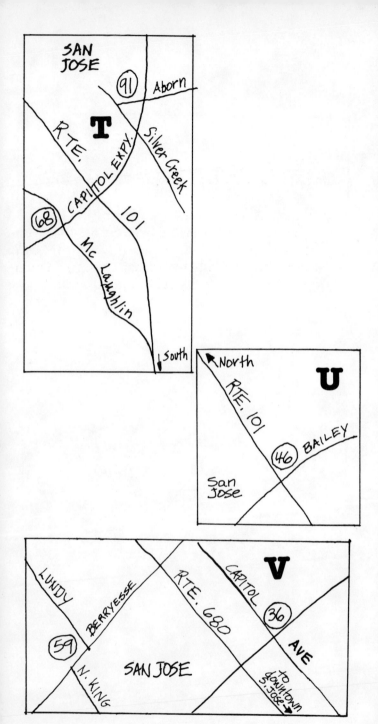

ACKNOWLEDGEMENTS

It is with great appreciation and gratitude that I acknowledge the following persons for their support, assistance, and encouragement: Nicholas W. Border, Lloyd and Michael Brazil, Norma Majumdar, Arlene Reed, and Debbie Thompson.

VALUE FINDER INDEX

CLOTHING

FLOOR COVERINGS

FOOD

HOME FURNISHERS

LINENS

LUGGAGE

OFFICE FURNITURE

WALL COVERINGS

Notes

Notes

Notes

Notes

Notes